Wedding Readings and Vows

Wedding Readings and Vows

for church and civil ceremonies

from **confetti.co.uk**
don't get married without us...

First published in 2003
by Octopus Publishing Group,
2–4 Heron Quays, London E14 4JP
www.conran-octopus.co.uk
Text copyright © 2003 Confetti Network
Readings and Poems © individual copyright holders
Book design and layout copyright
© 2003 Conran Octopus Limited
Illustrations copyright © Confetti Network

All rights reserved. No part of this book may be reproduced,
stored in a retrieval system, or transmitted, in any form
or by any means, electronic, electrostatic, magnetic tape,
mechanical, photocopying, recording or otherwise, without
prior permission in writing of the Publisher.
A catalogue record for this book is available from
the British Library.

Publishing Director Lorraine Dickey
Senior Editor Katey Day
Assistant Editor Sybella Marlow
Creative Director Leslie Harrington
Designer Jeremy Tilston
Senior Production Controller Manjit Sihra

Thanks also to the staff at Confetti.co.uk,
brides, grooms, guests and Aunt Betti

ISBN 1 84091 309 6
Printed in Europe

Other books in this series include *Wedding Planner;
Wedding Readings; How to Write a Wedding Speech;
Wedding Speeches; The Best Man's Wedding; The Bridesmaid's
Wedding; Your Daughter's Wedding* and *The Wedding Book of Calm*

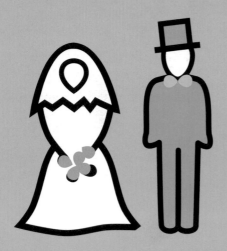

Contents

'I do.'

These two little words are seen as the cornerstone of the whole marriage ceremony, the logical conclusion of the three little words, 'I love you.'

So did you know that these two words are not actually included in a standard English, Welsh or Scottish ceremony? When the minister asks the bride and groom if they will take each other to be man and wife, the usual answer is 'I will'. The vows are, naturally, the most important part of the whole day, and you'll probably want to spend some time ensuring that they reflect what you really want to say. Even the standard wording will differ depending on whether you are having a religious or civil ceremony, or whether you have chosen an alternative such as a humanist, pagan or hand-fasting ceremony. Whereas some people are keen to follow the traditional age-old wording used by so many thousands of wedded couples over the centuries, others want to express something personal and individual, and put their own stamp on the proceedings. Whichever you prefer, you will find information and guidance in this book.

Readings at your ceremony can add meaning to the day. Wedding readings are by no means a necessary or legal part of the ceremony, but they enhance it and allow things to be said and thought about that are not explicit in the statutory words. Readings are also a great way to involve family and friends in the ceremony.

This book provides you with the very best of love and marriage poetry, prose and Bible readings, for secular and non-secular ceremonies, as well as some suitable for receptions.

The vows section guides you through the legalities of vows, providing a comprehensive guide to writing your own and also an inspirational selection of sample vows covering different situations.

Wedding readings

Readings loud and clear

Readings can add to the solemnity of an occasion, or provide a welcome moment of light relief. In civil weddings, they add colour and individuality to the formulaic; in religious venues, they provide a breath of worldliness that non-religious people can relate to. Above all, readings underline the importance of your day by articulating the deep values underlying your momentous decision to marry.

Readings are also a way of involving family and friends in your ceremony, giving them important and meaningful roles to play. If you want to involve children, there are a number of shorter readings, secular, religious and biblical, that are perfect for younger readers.

Church weddings

A Christian wedding ceremony generally follows this pattern. Usually a hymn is sung once everyone is in church. A reading may follow, then the vicar states the reason for the gathering and asks if anyone knows why the marriage should not take place.

Having received the couple's agreement to be married, the vicar asks who is giving the bride away. The bride's father, or escort, places her right hand in that of the vicar, who gives it to the groom.

The marriage vows are taken first by the groom and then the bride, led by the vicar. After the couple have exchanged rings, the vicar pronounces them man and wife (although the full legal requirements are not actually met until the marriage register has been signed).

Normally, the vicar will deliver a short sermon, one or two hymns are sung and prayers are said for the couple. Readings may also be appropriate here, before and after a hymn. At this point, the couple receive Holy Communion if they have chosen a communion service.

The bride and groom, followed by the best man, chief bridesmaid, their parents, bridesmaids, pages and any other witnesses, proceed behind the vicar to the vestry to sign the register.

At a given signal, the organist will strike up a piece of music, and the party leaves the church.

For a religious ceremony, you are usually offered a selection of biblical readings, but you may also have the option of reading out a secular text too.

Exactly how secular the text can be will depend on the church in question, but perhaps also on the minister. A traditional high Anglican vicar, for instance, might allow some Shakespeare, but draw the line at modern poetry, whereas a 'trendy vicar' might be happy to consider a much wider selection of texts. Both, however, would want to ensure that the readings do not undermine the Christian view of marriage, so always make sure that your choice is checked and approved by the minister.

What are my options?

Most services will include one or two readings. Ultimately, the choice of Bible text is yours, but you will probably want guidance and help, which clergy are always ready to provide.

Churches with a formal tradition of worship provide a choice of proposed texts. For Anglicans, the *Alternative Service Book* (ASB) carries a selection, and Roman Catholic couples are usually given a booklet with a fair-sized sample to choose from – although, again, you will usually be allowed to choose any text you wish from the Bible.

More informal churches, such as Baptists or Pentecostalists, may simply invite you to choose directly from the Bible, but will be happy to provide suggestions.

Choosing the perfect Bible reading

Even if you go for all-religious readings in your ceremony, there are still choices to make and decisions to take.

Choosing your theme

To help you decide on a suitable reading, it's a good idea to think about the sort of message you want your chosen words to convey. Though these can be surprisingly varied, three clear themes generally emerge:

Marriage blessed by God
Love is all you need
Hints for a happy life.

Marriage blessed by God

As you might expect, the most common readings chosen are texts from both Old and New Testaments that talk about marriage as being willed and blessed by God. Take, for instance, the passage from the creation story in Genesis, where God creates man:

'So God created man in his own image; in the image of God he created him; male and female he created them. God blessed them and said to them, "be fruitful and increase"...' (Genesis: 1:27, *New English Bible*)

Jesus himself quotes another passage from Genesis to make clear his own belief in marriage as a lifelong commitment:

'Some Pharisees came to him to test him. They asked, "Is it lawful for a man to divorce his wife for any and every reason?"
"Haven't you read," he replied, "that at the beginning the

Creator 'made them male and female,' and said, 'For this reason a man will leave his father and mother and be united to his wife, and the two will become one flesh'? So they are no longer two, but one. Therefore what God has joined together, let man not separate." (Matthew 19:3–6)

Love is all you need

Other popular choices come from the wealth of texts that offer insight into the nature of love itself. Top of the pops here has long been the famous Hymn to Love from the first letter of Saint Paul to the Corinthians, chapter 13. Many will remember Tony Blair reading it at Princess Diana's funeral.

Less well-known, though equally uplifting, are various passages about love from Saint John's Gospel and his letters:

'Jesus said: "As the Father has loved me, so have I loved you. Now remain in my love. If you obey my commands, you will remain in my love, just as I have obeyed my Father's commands and remain in his love. I have told you this so that my joy may be in you and your joy may be complete. My commandment is this: Love each another, as I have loved you. Greater love has no one than this that he lays down his life for his friends." (John 15:9–13)

Some might object that the love in question is divine love and not the human, passionate love that is being celebrated in marriage. But if anyone suggests this, you can remind them that for believers, the point of the marriage ceremony is that human love is made holy and raised to the divine level.

And just to prove that God does not disapprove of human love, the Bible contains a whole book of passionate love poetry, the Song of Songs. It is rarely chosen, and by today's standards seems rather quaint, yet for the fifth century BC, its verses have an unashamedly erotic ring:

> 'Arise, my love, my fair one come away. O my dove, in the clefts of the rock, in the covert of the cliff, let me see your face, let me hear your voice; for your voice is sweet, and your face is comely... My beloved is mine and I am his... Set me as a seal upon your heart, as a seal upon your arm; for love is strong as death, jealousy is cruel as the grave. Its flashes are flashes of fire, a most vehement flame. Many waters cannot quench love, neither can the floods drown it...' (Song of Songs 2:13–14,16; 8:6–7 Revised Standard Version).

Hints for a happy life

There's plenty of advice in the Good Book too about how to make your marriage a successful one, and no lack of texts on the moral obligations of marriage either. Of course, the ways in which biblical writers thought centuries ago may now seem rather outdated. Saint Paul, for instance, is often accused of male chauvinism, and his advice to the early Christians of Ephesus seems to bear this out:

> 'Give way to one another in obedience to Christ. Wives should regard their husbands as they regard the Lord, since as Christ is head of the Church and saves the whole body, so is a husband the head of his wife; and as the Church submits to Christ, so should wives to their husbands, in everything.' (Ephesians 5:21–24)

Modern commentators (including Pope John Paul II) claim that what Saint Paul really meant is that husband and wife should give way to one another, and indeed Paul goes on to say that the husband 'must love his wife as he loves himself' and sacrifice himself for her. Although few feminists will be satisfied by this answer, a large number of women still choose this text, so some at least are convinced. Eastern Orthodox couples have no choice in the matter, as in their tradition it is one of the two obligatory texts in the marriage service.

If you are looking for something less contentious, however, try the following:

> 'You are God's chosen race, his saints; he loves you, and you should be clothed in sincere compassion, in kindness and humility, gentleness and patience. Bear with one another; forgive each other as soon as a quarrel begins. The Lord has forgiven you; now you must do the same. Over all these clothes, to keep them together and complete them, put on love. And may the peace of Christ reign in your hearts, because it is for this that you were called together as parts of one body. Always be thankful.' (Colossians 3:12–15)

So whatever you're looking for, the Bible is a sufficiently vast resource for most people to find something to suit them. Remember that your priest or minister will be happy to help you, and if you're not very religious yourselves, don't hesitate to ask family or friends who may be more familiar with the book. Lastly, if you decide on a text outside those suggested to you, stick with your choice: the essential thing is that the readings you choose strike a chord with you.

Choosing your Bible version

It's not just a question of choosing your Bible reading. You can choose a Bible version – that is, a translation – too. There are many available today, each with its own style, and some couples will have a distinct preference.

Lovers of English literature may well wish to hear the beautiful phrases of the King James version, dating back to the 17th century; while others may find its language hopelessly old-fashioned and even incomprehensible.

Recent translations are more modern in their approach. The *Revised Standard Version* (RSV), for example, sticks as closely as possible to the traditional translations, while rendering them in modern English. Others, such as the *New English Bible* (NEB) or the *Good News Bible*, try to be more up to date – sometimes at the risk of sounding banal.

The selection of readings given in the Anglican ASB is chosen from several versions, while Roman Catholics in general use the *Jerusalem Bible*, which is now available in an even more updated version using 'gender-inclusive language'. To give you an idea of what is at stake, compare these versions of an extract from St Paul's famous passage on love, quoted first in the King James version and then NEB-style.

King James version

'Charity suffereth long, and is kind; charity envieth not; charity vaunteth not itself, is not puffed up, doth not behave itself unseemly, seeketh not her own, is not easily provoked, thinketh no evil; rejoiceth not in iniquity, but rejoiceth in the truth; beareth all things, believeth all things, hopeth all things, endureth all things.'

New English Bible

'Love is patient; love is kind and envies no one. Love is never boastful, nor conceited, nor rude; never selfish, nor quick to take offence. Love keeps no score of wrongs; does not gloat over other men's sins, but delights in the truth. There is nothing love cannot face; there is no limit to its faith, its hope, and its endurance.' (I Corinthians 13:4–7)

Chapter and verse

To help you find Bible quotations, a simple system known as 'chapter and verse' is used. Here's how it works. The Bible is divided into a series of books, contained in the Old and New Testaments. A biblical quotation is identified by the name of the book, often abbreviated (e.g. Gen for Genesis, or Matt or Mt for the Gospel according to Saint Matthew). Then you'll see two numbers. The first represents the chapter number of that particular book, the second points to the verses referred to (these are the small numbers which divide the text inside each chapter). So, for instance, Gen.1,16 would mean the sixteenth verse of the first chapter of the book of Genesis. To help your search, you'll find a table at the front of your Bible giving the order of the books and their abbreviations.

Civil weddings

Nearly half of all weddings in the UK nowadays are solemnized in civil ceremonies. As civil weddings don't have the elements of hymns and a sermon that anglican weddings include, readings tend to assume a great deal of importance on these occasions.

That apart, the order of service is very similar to that of an anglican ceremony:

Entrance music for bride
Introduction
Reading (optional)
The Marriage
Reading (optional)
Signing of the register
Reading (optional)
Exit music

At a register office wedding, you don't need to have any readings and you must obtain prior approval to use any. Similarly, in weddings that take place in state-licensed venues, a registrar will need to approve your choice of readings. Remember too, that civil weddings do not allow for any material with a religious content. Obviously this rules out biblical texts and hymns, but also more loosely spiritual material such as *The Prophet* or *Desiderata*.

If you want more freedom in the content of your ceremony, you might consider an alternative such as a humanist wedding. Here you'll have much greater flexibility to choose the readings you want, or – if you wish – you may even be able to write your own.

Generally, you are allowed to choose who does the readings on the day. This is often a useful way of including in your ceremony a close friend or relative whom you weren't able to choose as an usher or bridesmaid, or who lives too far away to be able to be more involved in the preparations.

Choosing non-religious readings

Once you've established how much scope your chosen ceremony allows, it's time to think about specific non-religious readings that you could include in your service. In theory, they could be any suitable extract from a work of literature, non-fiction or poetry. Here are a few pointers to get you started:

- Do you or your partner have a favourite poet, author or passage of writing that might be suitable?

- Look in books of quotations under headings such as 'love' and 'marriage'. Note any particular quotations or authors that you find appealing and look into them more closely. The Internet is a valuable tool for finding the author or full text of a piece you like.

- Keep your eye out for unusual sources. Children's books, for example *Guess How Much I Love You* or extracts from *Winnie the Pooh,* are often good starting points. If you wish to reproduce your reading (for instance, in an order of service), you will need to make sure that it is out of copyright or that you obtain permission from the copyright holder, so bear this in mind while searching for your perfect piece.

- Try dipping into this book or *Wedding Readings*, also in this series, and reading out interesting bits to each other.

- Your register office may provide a booklet that contains a selection of readings approved for use in civil ceremonies.

- The British Humanist Association's guide to non-religious wedding ceremonies *Sharing the Future*, has a chapter on readings with several interesting suggestions. Order through www.humanism.org.uk or call 020 7430 0908.

Spoilt for choice

As you will discover, the range of material available is
enormous. Poetry is a good option, its language well suited
to the significance of the occasion. The more traditional
might go for something from Shakespeare. Sonnet 116 ('Let
me not to the marriage of true minds admit impediments...')
is a popular choice, as are these lines from Hamlet:

Doubt thou the stars are fire;
Doubt that the sun doth move;
Doubt truth to be a liar;
But never doubt I love.

Modern poetry offers some fine possibilities too, including
TS Eliot's 'A Dedication to My Wife', WH Auden's 'O tell me
the truth about love', and Adrian Henri's 'Without You'.
'Poem' by DH Lawrence is another favourite, with its
evocation of coupledom as 'the gem of mutual peace
emerging from the wild chaos of love'.

If you'd rather go for prose, there are some wonderful older passages, such as Thomas à Kempis's 14th-century meditation ('Love feels no burden, thinks nothing of trouble, attempts what is above its strength, pleads no excuse of impossibility...'). Or for the more modern-minded, there are such gems as the famous extract from Albert Schweitzer's autobiography ('We must not try to force our way into the personality of another'), or the thoughts of Paul Kurtz: 'A successful marriage is one where each partner discovers that it is better to give love than to receive it'.

Further afield, there are plenty of texts from other traditions that may suit. Kahlil Gibran's evocation of marriage in *The Prophet* is a very popular choice. But you'll also come across Eskimo love songs and French symbolist poets (take a look at translations of Paul Eluard's beautiful poems), African Bushman lyrics and native American texts. This Apache blessing, for instance, is now frequently used:

Now you will feel no rain,
For each of you will be shelter to the other.
Now you will feel no cold,
For each of you will be warmth to the other.
Now there is no more loneliness for you,
For each of you will be companion to the other.
Now you are two bodies,
But there is only one life before you.
Go now to your dwelling place,
To enter into the days of your togetherness.
And may your days be good and long upon the earth.'

What all these suggestions have in common is a celebration of married life in all its fullness and variety. The best readings celebrate not just the first flash of passion, but all the enduring qualities of marriage too: fidelity, companionship, mutual fulfilment, security and serenity. Another good choice is James Dillet Freeman's 'Blessing For A Marriage':

'May you always need one another – not so much to fill your emptiness, as to help you to know your fullness...'

More non-religious readings

Just how can you find the right words to encapsulate both the feelings you have for each other and the significance of the day in a concise, to-the-point style?

Poetry might be just the thing, but most people don't tend to come across it on a daily basis. Here are some more equally appropriate though less well-known ideas to add an individual touch to your unique day.

Going back through the centuries, the last three stanzas of Tennyson's 'Maud' are perfect, as is a selection of verses from Spenser's 'Epithalamion'. Alternatively, Christina Rossetti's 'A Birthday' is a good length and ends, 'the birthday of my life is come, my love is come to me'. Great stuff! You'll find all of these in major bookshops.

The twentieth century has seen a multitude of poets and novelists writing on the age-old theme. If you can get past his strange punctuation, e. e. cummings' 'I carry your heart with me (I carry it in/my heart)' is a stunning choice, and his *Selected Poems 1923–1958* is readily available. The images he uses are wonderful – there are no clichés and it's the perfect length for a reading. William Carlos Williams' 'The Ivy Crown' is just gorgeous, and is, again, a suitable length. His *Collected Poems* are also easy to get hold of.

Brian Patten's *Love Poems* is one of the most moving collections of the past few years. Have a look at Eithne Strong's 'Dedication' in the recent *Irish Love Poems*, which starts, 'To you / I have given. / I want to be with you / along the way you have chosen.' This book is a real treasure trove of poems.

Or how about some song lyrics? These are becoming more and more popular with couples – it adds a twist to the more conventional reading and songwriters often manage to say things in truly original ways. Ozzy Ozbourne should be avoided perhaps, but have a look at Joni Mitchell's lyrics and poems for some ethereal stuff that encapsulates it all.

For great prose, try the ending of James Joyce's *Ulysses* for size. You'll have to be careful to avoid the racier bits, but it's an incredible monologue and sums up all the passion, love and commitment in the world (and you don't have to plough through the whole book – it's right there in the last ten pages!). Here's a sample: 'I put my arms around him yes and drew him down to me so he could feel my breasts all perfume yes and his heart was going like mad and yes I said yes I will Yes.' It's an intrepid reader who will be willing to take this on, however, and it's not appropriate for the more conventional wedding venues. You'll have to choose someone who will perform rather than read this piece, but it'll be well worth it – it's a showstopper.

If you want a further selection beyond what you'll find here, try the anthologies. Among the best are *Love Poetry Across the Centuries*, and *A Book of Prayers for the First Years of Marriage*. You're guaranteed to find something to suit all tastes. Choose readings that show the many facets of love and marriage – if you're going to use someone else's words to convey what the day means to you, make sure they're absolutely spot on!

Making a final decision

- Does the reading meet with approval from your minister?

- Is the text really about marriage and not just about falling in love?

- Will it fit in with the rest of the order of service? Is it a good foil for any other readings or prayers you've chosen?

- Is it a self-contained piece that needs no further explanation?

- Is it free of any material that might offend guests?

- Is it the right length? A reading that's too short may easily get drowned out by a coughing fit or crying baby, while a text that's too long may unbalance your whole ceremony.

- Will your chosen reader be able to handle the words?

Readings for a
church ceremony

Our selection of readings is not necessarily limited to those of the Anglican or even Christian tradition, but includes many which celebrate all aspects of spirituality and love.

The pieces we have collected here represent some of the most enduring pieces of romantic poetry and prose ever written, with sentiments as valid and meaningful to couples now as they have been over many hundreds of years. The writings of Dante from the 13th century and the words of 14th century poet Thomas à Kempis still encapsulate many couples' thoughts and emotions about their union.

Readings aren't necessarily just for the ceremony. If you can't choose between readings, or don't want to include them in your marriage, then why not consider having them at your reception? A reading before the wedding breakfast or to introduce the speeches makes a great personal touch.

There are also some beautiful readings that are suitable to be spoken by the couple who have just married, or for other members of the family, and we've included a selection of these here.

For more inspiration and readings, see the accompanying volume to this, *Wedding Readings*.

When you have selected your ideal reading, check whether it is still in copyright. If it is, you cannot reproduce it (for instance, in an order of service) without obtaining permission from the copyright holder.

Perfect Woman
William Wordsworth (1770–1850)

She was a phantom of delight
When first she gleam'd upon my sight;
A lovely apparition, sent
To be a moment's ornament;
Her eyes as stars of twilight fair;
Like twilight's, too, her dusky hair;
But all things else about her drawn
From May-time and the cheerful dawn;
A dancing shape, an image gay,
To haunt, to startle, and waylay.
I saw her upon nearer view,
A Spirit, yet a Woman too!
Her household motions light and free,
And steps of virgin liberty;
A countenance in which did meet
Sweet records, promises as sweet:
A creature not too bright or good
For human nature's daily food;
For transient sorrows, simple wiles,
Praise, blame, love, kisses, tears and smiles.
And now I see with eye serene
The very pulse of the machine;
A being breathing thoughtful breath,
A traveller between life and death;
The reason firm, the temperate will,
Endurance, foresight, strength, and skill;
A perfect Woman, nobly plann'd,
To warn, to comfort, and command;
And yet a Spirit still, and bright
With something of angelic light.

Love Lives
John Clare (1793–1864)

Love lives beyond
The tomb, the earth, which fades like dew.
I love the fond,
The faithful, and the true

Love lives in sleep,
The happiness of healthy dreams
Eve's dews may weep,
But love delightful seems.

'Tis heard in Spring
When light and sunbeams, warm and kind,
On angels' wing
Bring love and music to the mind.

And where is voice,
So young, so beautiful and sweet
As nature's choice,
Where Spring and lovers meet?

Love lives beyond
The tomb, the earth, the flowers, and dew.
I love the fond,
The faithful, young and true.

So, we'll go no more a-roving
Lord Byron (1788–1824)

So, we'll go no more a-roving
So late into the night,
Though the heart be still as loving,
And the moon be still as bright.

For the sword outweighs its sheath,
And the soul wears out the breast,
And the heart must pause to breathe,
And love itself have rest.

Though the night was made for loving,
And the day returns too soon,
Yet we'll go no more a-roving,
By the light of the moon.

Extract from De Imitatio Christi
Thomas à Kempis (1379–1471)

Love is a mighty power, a great and complete good.
Love alone lightens every burden, and makes rough places smooth.
It bears every hardship as though it were nothing, and renders all
bitterness sweet and acceptable.

Nothing is sweeter than love,
Nothing stronger,
Nothing higher,
Nothing wider,
Nothing more pleasant,
Nothing fuller or better in heaven or earth; for love is born of God.

Love flies, runs and leaps for joy.
It is free and unrestrained.
Love knows no limits, but ardently transcends all bounds.
Love feels no burden, takes no account of toil,
Attempts things beyond its strength.

My Delight and thy Delight
Robert Bridges (1844–1930)

My delight and thy delight
Walking, like two angels white,
In the gardens of the night:

My desire and thy desire
Twining to a tongue of fire,
Leaping live, and laughing higher:

Thro' the everlasting strife
In the mysteries of life.
Love, from whom the world begun,
Hath the secret of the sun.

Love can tell, and love alone,
Whence the million stars were strewn,
Why each atom knows its own,
How, in spite of woe and death,
Gay is life, and sweet is breath:

This he taught us, this we knew,
Happy in his science true,
Hand in hand as we stood
'Neath the shadows of the wood,
Heart to heart as we lay
In the dawning of the day.

Friendship
Hartley Coleridge (1796–1849)

When we were idlers with the loitering rills,
The need of human love we little noted:
Our love was nature; and the peace that floated
On the white mist,
And dwelt upon the hills,
To sweet accord subdued our wayward wills:
One soul was ours, one mind, one heart devoted,
That, wisely doting, ask'd not why it doted,
And ours the unknown joy, which knowing kills.
But now I find how dear thou wert to me;
That man is more than half of nature's treasure,
Of that fair beauty which no eye can see,
Of that sweet music which no ear can measure;
And now the streams may sing for others' pleasure,
The hills sleep on in their eternity.

Love's Philosophy
Percy Bysshe Shelley (1792–1822)

The fountains mingle with the rivers
And the rivers with the oceans,
The winds of heaven mix forever
With a sweet emotion;
Nothing in the world is single;
All things by a law divine
In one spirit meet and mingle.
Why not I with thine?

See the mountains kiss high heaven
And the waves clasp one another;
No sister-flower would be forgiven
If it disdained its brother,
And the sunlight clasps the earth
And the moonbeams kiss the sea:
What is all this sweet work worth
If thou kiss not me?

Never Marry but for Love
William Penn (1644–1718)

Never marry but for love; but see that thou lovest what is lovely. He that minds a body and not a soul has not the better part of that relationship, and will consequently lack the noblest comfort of a married life.

Between a man and his wife nothing ought to rule but love. As love ought to bring them together, so it is the best way to keep them well together.

A husband and wife that love one another show their children that they should do so too. Others visibly lose their authority in their families by their contempt of one another, and teach their children to be unnatural by their own examples.

Let not enjoyment lessen, but augment, affection; it being the basest of passions to like when we have not, what we slight when we possess.

Here it is we ought to search out our pleasure, where the field is large and full of variety, and of an enduring nature; sickness, poverty or disgrace being not able to shake it because it is not under the moving influences of worldly contingencies.

Nothing can be more entire and without reserve; nothing more zealous, affectionate and sincere; nothing more contented than such a couple, nor greater temporal felicity than to be one of them.

Love Rules the Court
Sir Walter Scott (1771–1832)

Love rules the court,
The camp, the grove,
And men below, and the saints above,
For love is heaven
and heaven is love.

To be one with each other
George Eliot (1819–1880)

What greater thing is there for two human souls than to
feel that they are joined together to strengthen each other
in all labour, to minister to each other in all sorrow, to share
with each other in all gladness, to be one with each other in
the silent unspoken memories?

The Prophet
Kahlil Gibran (1883–1931)

Your friend is your needs answered. He is your field which you sow with love and reap with thanksgiving. And he is your board and your fireside. For you come to him with your hunger, and you seek him for peace.

When your friend speaks his mind you fear not the 'nay' in your own mind, nor do you withhold the 'aye'. And when he is silent your heart ceases not to listen to his heart; For without words, in friendship, all thoughts, all desires, all expectations are born and shared, with joy that is unclaimed.

When you part from your friend, you grieve not; for that which you love most in him may be clearer in his absence, as the mountain to the climber is clearer from the plain.

And let there be no purpose in friendship save the deepening of the spirit. For love that seeks aught but the disclosure of its own mystery is not love but a net cast forth: and only the unprofitable is caught.

And let your best be for your friend. If he must know the ebb of your tide, let him know its flood also. For what is your friend that you should seek him with hours to kill? Seek him always with hours to live. For it is his to fill your need, but not your emptiness. And in the sweetness of friendship let there be laughter, and sharing of pleasures. For in the dew of little things the heart finds its morning and is refreshed.

One day I wrote her name upon the strand
Edmund Spenser (1552–1599)

One day I wrote her name upon the strand,
But came the waves and washed it away:
Again I wrote it with a second hand,
But came the tide, and made my pains his prey.
Vain man, said she, that dost in vain assay
A mortal thing so to immortalize!
For I myself shall like to this decay,
And eke my name be wiped out likewise.
Not so (quoth I), let baser things devise
To die in dust, but you shall live by fame:
My verse your virtues rare shall eternize,
And in the heavens write your glorious name:
Where, whenas Death shall all the world subdue,
Our love shall live, and later life renew.

On Marriage
Kahlil Gibran (1883–1931)

Then Almitra spoke again and said, 'And what of Marriage, master?'
And he answered saying:
You were born together, and together you shall be forevermore.
You shall be together when white wings of death scatter your days.
Aye, you shall be together even in the silent memory of God.
But let there be spaces in your togetherness,
And let the winds of the heavens dance between you.

Love one another but make not a bond of love:
Let it rather be a moving sea between the shores of your souls.
Fill each other's cup but drink not from one cup.
Give one another of your bread but eat not from the same loaf.
Sing and dance together and be joyous, but let each one of you
be alone,
Even as the strings of a lute are alone though they quiver with the
same music.

Give your hearts, but not into each other's keeping.
For only the hand of Life can contain your hearts.
And stand together, yet not too near together:
For the pillars of the temple stand apart,
And the oak tree and the cypress grow not in each other's shadow.

Truth and Beauty
John Hogben

Two souls there are in nature and in life –
The soul of Beauty and the soul of Truth;
Towards which we yearn and strain with restless strife,
Along paths fraught with malice or with ruth; –
In the red face of ridicule and scorn,
Men sought, and still must seek these – or within,
(In spite of all earth's sorrow and her sin),
The soul is to search and manner born.
And still, in looking Beauty in the face,
With strong prophetic joy we recognise
Something of what we may be, as we trace
Our own dim shadow in her lustrous eyes;
Nor may we part such with a dull harsh rule –
Beauty is true and Truth is beautiful!

True Woman – her Love
Dante Gabriel Rossetti (1828–1882)

She loves him; for her infinite soul is Love,
And he her lode-star. Passion in her is
A glass facing his fire, where the bright bliss
Is mirrored, and the heat returned. Yet move
That glass, a stranger's amorous flame to prove,
And it shall turn, by instant contraries,
Ice to the moon; while her pure fire to his
For whom it burns, clings close I' the heart's alcove.

Lo! they are one. With wifely breast to breast
And circling arms, she welcomes all command
Of love, – her soul to answering ardours fann'd:
Yet as morn springs or twilight sinks to rest,
Ah! who shall say she deems not loveliest
The hour of sisterly sweet hand-in-hand?

Extract from **Sonnets from the Portuguese**
Elizabeth Barrett Browning (1806–1861)

How do I love thee? Let me count the ways.
I love thee to the depth and breadth and height
My soul can reach, when feeling out of sight
For the ends of Being and ideal Grace.
I love thee to the level of every day's
Most quiet need, by sun and candle light.
I love thee freely, as men strive for Right;
I love thee purely, as they turn from Praise.
I love thee with the passion put to use
In my old griefs, and with my childhood's faith.

I love thee with a love I seemed to lose
With my lost saints, – I love thee with the breath,
Smiles, tears, of all my life! – and, if God choose,
I shall but love thee better after death.

Two Lovers II
Mary F. Robinson

I have another lover loving me,
Himself beloved of all men, fair and true.
He would not have me change altho' I grew
Perfect as Light, because more tenderly
He loves myself than loves what I might be.
Low at my feet he sings the winter through,
And, never won, I love to hear him woo.
For in my heaven both sun and moon is he,
To my bare life a fruitful-flooding Nile,
His voice like April airs that in our isle
Wake sap in trees that slept since autumn went.
His words are all caresses, and his smile
The relic of some Eden Ravishment;
And he that loves me so I call: Content.

Extracts from *Romeo and Juliet*
William Shakespeare (1564–1616)

Love is a smoke made with the fume of sighs;
Being purg'd, a fire sparkling in lovers' eyes;
Being vex'd, a sea nourish'd with lovers' tears;
What is it else? A madness most discreet,
A choking gall, and a preserving sweet.
(Act I.i)

O, she doth teach the torches to burn bright!
Her beauty hangs upon the cheek of night
Like a rich jewel in an Ethiop's ear;
Beauty too rich for use, for earth too dear!
So shows a snowy dove trooping with crows,
As yonder lady o'er her fellows shows.
The measure done, I'll watch her place of stand,
And, touching hers, make blessed my rude hand.
Did my heart love till now? Forswear it, sight!
For I ne'er saw true beauty till this night.
(Act I.v)

But soft! What light through yonder window breaks?
It is the East and Juliet is the sun!
Arise, fair sun, and kill the envious moon,
Who is already sick and pale with grief
That thou her maid art more fair than she.
Be not her maid, since she is envious.
Her vestal livery is but sick and green,
And none but fools do wear it. Cast it off.
It is my lady; O it is my love!
O that she knew she were!
She speaks, yet she says nothing. What of that?
Her eye discourses; I will answer it.
I am too bold; 'tis not to me she speaks.
Two of the fairest stars in all the heaven,
Having some business, do entreat her eyes
To twinkle in their spheres till they return.
What if her eyes were there, they in her head?
The brightness of her cheek would shame those stars
As daylight doth a lamp; her eyes in heaven
Would through the airy region stream so bright
That birds would sing and think it were not night.
See how she leans her cheek upon her hand!
O that I were a glove upon that hand,
That I might touch that cheek!
(Act II.ii)

Sonnet 18
William Shakespeare (1564–1616)

Shall I compare thee to a summer's day?
Thou art more lovely and more temperate:
Rough winds do shake the darling buds of May,
And summer's lease hath all too short a date.
Sometimes too hot the eye of heaven shines,
And often is his gold complexion dimm'd;
And every fair from fair sometimes declines,
By chance, or nature's changing course untrimm'd;
But the eternal summer shall not fade,
Nor lose possession of that fair thou ow'st,
Nor shall death brag thou wander'st in his shade,
When eternal lines to time thou grow'st,
So long as men can breathe, or eyes can see,
So long lives this, and this gives life to thee.

Sonnet 116
William Shakespeare (1564–1616)

Let me not to the marriage of true minds
Admit impediments. Love is not love
Which alters when it alteration finds,
Or bends with the remover to remove:
O, no! it is an ever-fixed mark,
That looks on tempests and is never shaken;
It is the star to every wand'ring bark,
Whose worth's unknown, although his height be taken.

Love's not Time's fool, though rosy lips and cheeks
Within his bending sickle's compass come;
Love alters not with his brief hours and weeks,
But bears it out even to the edge of doom.
If this be error and upon me prov'd,
I never writ, nor no man ever lov'd.

Bible readings

Choosing biblical readings is both exciting and daunting, because of the sheer volume of passages. Although some pieces may leap into your head immediately, and many more can be found here, it's a good idea to take some time to browse through whichever version of the Bible you prefer and just think about which passages speak to you, and to your guests. You can even use the extracts in this book as a quick guide, and then follow them up in your Bible or with your minister, enlarging or cutting the passage to suit the mood of your ceremony.

Our listing of scripture readings has been separated into three sections: the New Testament, the Old Testament and the Psalms. As with all readings and poems that you wish to include in your wedding service, you must discuss them with your minister first and obtain approval.

The New Testament

Matthew 5: 1–10
The Beatitudes

1 Now when he saw the crowds, he went up on a mountainside and sat down. His disciples came to him,
2 and he began to teach them, saying:
3 'Blessed are the poor in spirit, for theirs is the kingdom of heaven.
4 Blessed are those who mourn, for they will be comforted.
5 Blessed are the meek, for they will inherit the earth.
6 Blessed are those who hunger and thirst for righteousness, for they will be filled.
7 Blessed are the merciful, for they will be shown mercy.
8 Blessed are the pure in heart, for they will see God.
9 Blessed are the peacemakers, for they will be called sons of God.
10 Blessed are those who are persecuted because of righteousness, for theirs is the kingdom of heaven.'

Matthew 7: 24–29
A wise man built his house upon a rock

24 'Therefore everyone who hears these words of mine and puts them into practice is like a wise man who built his house on the rock.

25 The rain came down, the streams rose, and the winds blew and beat against that house; yet it did not fall, because it had its foundation on the rock.

26 But everyone who hears these words of mine and does not put them into practice is like a foolish man who built his house on sand.

27 The rain came down, the streams rose, and the winds blew and beat against that house, and it fell with a great crash.'

28 When Jesus had finished saying these things, the crowds were amazed at his teaching,

29 because he taught as one who had authority, and not as their teachers of the law.

I Corinthians 13: 4–13

Love

4 Love is patient, love is kind. It does not envy, it does not boast, it is not proud.

5 It is not rude, it is not self-seeking, it is not easily angered, it keeps no record of wrongs.

6 Love does not delight in evil but rejoices with the truth.

7 It always protects, always trusts, always hopes, always perseveres.

8 Love never fails. But where there are prophecies, they will cease; where there are tongues, they will be stilled; where there is knowledge, it will pass away.

9 For we know in part and we prophesy in part,

10 but when perfection comes, the imperfect disappears.

11 When I was a child, I talked like a child, I thought like a child, I reasoned like a child. When I became a man, I put childish ways behind me.

12 Now we see but a poor reflection as in a mirror; then we shall see face to face. Now I know in part; then I shall know fully, even as I am fully known.

13 And now these three remain: faith, hope and love. But the greatest of these is love.

Ephesians 5: 21–33

Wives submit to your husbands, husbands love your wives

21 Submit to one another out of reverence for Christ.

22 Wives, submit to your husbands as to the Lord.

23 For the husband is the head of the wife as Christ is the head of the church, his body, of which he is the Saviour.

24 Now as the church submits to Christ, so also wives should submit to their husbands in everything.

25 Husbands, love your wives, just as Christ loved the church and gave himself up for her

26 to make her holy, cleansing her by the washing with water through the word,

27 and to present her to himself as a radiant church, without stain or wrinkle or any other blemish, but holy and blameless.

28 In this same way, husbands ought to love their wives as their own bodies. He who loves his wife loves himself.

29 After all, no one ever hated his own body, but he feeds and cares for it, just as Christ does the church –

30 for we are members of his body.

31 'For this reason a man will leave his father and mother and be united to his wife, and the two will become one flesh.'

32 This is a profound mystery – but I am talking about Christ and the church.

33 However, each one of you also must love his wife as he loves himself, and the wife must respect her husband.

Other New Testament references:

Reference	Theme
Matthew 5: 13–16	You are the light of the world
Matthew 6: 19–21	Where your treasure is, there will your heart be also
Matthew 22: 36–40	The greatest commandment
Mark 10: 6–9	What God has joined together let no man put asunder
John 2: 1–12	Jesus's first miracle at the wedding in Cana
John 15: 1–8	I am the vine and you are the branches
John 15: 9–17	Love one another as I have loved you
Romans 12: 9–12	Let love be genuine
Ephesians 3: 14–19	May you be grounded and rooted in love
Colossians 3: 12–17	Put on love, which binds everything together in harmony
I John 4: 7–8, 12	Beloved, let us love one another
Revelation 19: 5–9	The marriage of the Lamb

The Old Testament

Genesis 1: 26–28
Male and female, He created them

26 Then God said, 'Let us make man in our image, in our likeness, and let him rule over the fish of the sea and the birds of the air, over the livestock, over all the earth, and over all the creatures that move along the ground.'
27 So God created man in his own image, in the image of God he created him; male and female he created them.
28 God blessed them and said to them, 'Be fruitful and increase in number; fill the earth and subdue it. Rule over the fish of the sea and the birds of the air and over every living creature that moves on the ground.'

Ecclesiastes 3: 1–8

For everything there is a season

1 There is a time for everything, and a season for every activity under heaven:

2 a time to be born and a time to die, a time to plant and a time to uproot,

3 a time to kill and a time to heal, a time to tear down and a time to build,

4 a time to weep and a time to laugh, a time to mourn and a time to dance,

5 a time to scatter stones and a time to gather them, a time to embrace and a time to refrain,

6 a time to search and a time to give up, a time to keep and a time to throw away,

7 a time to tear and a time to mend, a time to be silent and a time to speak,

8 a time to love and a time to hate, a time for war and a time for peace.

Isaiah 54: 10–14

My steadfast love will not depart from you

10 Though the mountains be shaken
and the hills be removed,
yet my unfailing love for you will not be shaken
nor my covenant of peace be removed,'
says the Lord, who has compassion on you.

11 'O afflicted city, lashed by storms and not comforted,
I will build you with stones of turquoise,
your foundations with sapphires.

12 I will make your battlements of rubies,
your gates of sparkling jewels,
and all your walls of precious stones.

13 All your sons will be taught by the Lord,
and great will be your children's peace.

14 In righteousness you will be established:
Tyranny will be far from you;
you will have nothing to fear.
Terror will be far removed;
it will not come near you.

Proverbs 31: 25–31

A good wife is more precious than jewels

25 She is clothed with strength and dignity;
   she can laugh at the days to come.
26 She speaks with wisdom,
   and faithful instruction is on her tongue.
27 She watches over the affairs of her household
   and does not eat the bread of idleness.
28 Her children arise and call her blessed;
   her husband also, and he praises her:
29 'Many women do noble things,
   but you surpass them all.'
30 Charm is deceptive, and beauty is fleeting;
   but a woman who fears the Lord is to be praised.
31 Give her the reward she has earned,
   and let her works bring her praise at the city gate.

Other Old Testament references:

Reference	Theme
Genesis 2: 20–24	Creation of woman
Genesis 9: 8–17	The rainbow and God's covenant with Noah
Joshua 24: 15	As for me and my house we will serve the Lord
Ruth 1: 16–17	Wither thou goest I will go
Ecclesiastes 4: 9–12	Two are better than one
Proverbs 3: 1-6, 13–18	Let not loyalty and faithfulness forsake you
Proverbs 31: 10–12	A good wife is more precious than jewels
Isaiah 30: 21	This is the way, walk in it
Isaiah 32: 2,16–18	Each will be like a hiding place, like streams in dry land
Isaiah 61: 10–11	Clothed in salvation... as a bride adorns herself with her jewels
Jeremiah 33: 10–11	There will be heard once more the voices of the bride and bridegroom
Hosea 2: 19–20	I will betroth you to me forever

Psalms

Psalm 95: 1–7
Let us sing to the Lord

1 Come, let us sing for joy to the Lord;
let us shout aloud to the Rock of our salvation.
2 Let us come before him with thanksgiving and extol him
with music and song.
3 For the Lord is the great God, the great King above
all gods.
4 In his hand are the depths of the earth, and the mountain
peaks belong to him.
5 The sea is his, for he made it, and his hands formed the
dry land.
6 Come, let us bow down in worship, let us kneel before
the Lord our Maker;
7 for he is our God and we are the people of his pasture,
the flock under his care.

Psalm 136: 1–9

His steadfast love endures forever

1 Give thanks to the Lord, for he is good.
His love endures forever.

2 Give thanks to the God of gods.
His love endures forever.

3 Give thanks to the Lord of lords:
His love endures forever.

4 to him who alone does great wonders,
His love endures forever.

5 who by his understanding made the heavens,
His love endures forever.

6 who spread out the earth upon the waters,
His love endures forever.

7 who made the great lights –
His love endures forever.

8 the sun to govern the day,
His love endures forever.

9 the moon and stars to govern the night;
His love endures forever.

Other Psalm references:

Reference	Theme
Psalm 8	O Lord, how majestic is thy name.
Psalm 34: 1–3	Let us exalt his name together.
Psalm 67	May God be gracious to us and bless us...
Psalm 100	Make a joyful noise to the Lord.
Psalm 121	He will keep your going out and your coming in.
Psalm 127	Unless the Lord builds the house...
Psalm 128	May you see your children's children!
Psalm 150	Praise the Lord!

Prayers

Father,
as we celebrate the marriage of ____ and ____ ,
strengthen our love for those close to us;
let us share the wonder of creation out of your love,
and your presence in our world.
Allow ____ and ____ to enjoy the commitment they have made to
each other and grant us happiness as we share in their joy – Amen.

Eternal God,
as we share in this joyful occasion,
Bless us and ____ and ____ as we pray
that they will love and care for each other
for the rest of their lives.
Bless this wedding
and the gifts of love and happiness it brings to us all – Amen.

God of love, creator of heaven and earth,
we praise you for your love and strength,
and for the wonderful gift of marriage.

We pray for ____ and ____, for their love for each other,
and for all the joy brought through the alliance of marriage.

We thank you for your love and commitment,
and we thank you for your guidance of ___ and ___
through their preparation for marriage.

Lord God, help ___ and ___ be loyal and faithful,
let them support each other through life.

Let them share their joys and burdens,
and help them honour the vows
that they have made to each other today.

Help them be wise in their decisions,
honest with each other,
and kind and loving to the people who support them.

Help ___ and ___ grow strong together,
and let them enjoy the experience of love forever
until their lives shall end – Amen.

Our Father,
may your love strengthen and support us,
and your wisdom deepen our knowledge.

Let your love guide us in our everyday lives
as we take on new challenges,
through Jesus Christ our Lord – Amen.

God of love,
we pray for ___ and ___ on this day
as they make the commitment of marriage
on this joyful occasion.

Guide them through their decisions
and support them in their choices.
Bless their children and allow them to enjoy your blessing
and serve your world – Amen.

This prayer is suitable for second marriages and for those with children

Father, we thank you for your blessing of this family,
Allowing these parents to share new joy with one another.
We pray for them to enjoy a happy life
and bless their children and their children's children.
Help them remain true to one another;
Grant them true love and happiness forever more – Amen.

(To be said by the couple)

God of love and strength,
We thank you for your blessing today,
and for your guidance that has led our paths to cross.

Guide us in our decisions through our marriage,
in good, bad, stability and change.

Help us support each other, be worthy of each other,
and protect and care for us and our home.

We trust and believe in you, now and forever
For the rest of our lives
Through Jesus Christ our Lord – Amen.

Readings for a civil ceremony

The joy of love and marriage has been a focus of literature and narrative tradition since people started putting their thoughts and feelings into words.

The passages of poetry and prose we have collected here represent some of the best and most popular pieces written in all corners of the world over the last 800 years.

While some are by such celebrated authors as Lord Byron and Wordsworth, many are traditional love poems or have been handed down for so many generations that their original author is now unknown.

For more inspiration and readings, see the accompanying volume to this, *Wedding Readings*.

When you have selected your ideal reading, check whether it is still in copyright. If it is, you cannot reproduce it (for instance, printed in an order of service) without first obtaining permission from the copyright holder.

She Walks in Beauty
Lord Byron (1788–1824)

She walks in beauty, like the night
Of cloudless climes and starry skies;
And all that's best of dark and bright
Meet in her aspect and her eyes:
Thus mellowed to that tender light
Which heaven to gaudy day denies.

One shade the more, one ray the less,
Had half impaired the nameless grace
Which waves in every raven tress,
Or softly lightens o'er her face;
Where thoughts serenely sweet express
How pure, how dear their dwelling place.

And on that cheek, and o'er that brow,
So soft, so calm, yet eloquent,
The smiles that win, the tints that glow,
But tell of days in goodness spent,
A mind at peace with all below,
A heart whose love is innocent!

Her Face
Arthur Gorges (1557–1625)

Her face
so fair
first bent
mine eye

Her tongue
so sweet
then drew
mine ear

Her wit
so sharp
then hit
my heart

Mine eye
to like
her face
doth lead

Mine ear
to learn
her tongue
doth teach

My heart
to love
her wit
doth move

Her face
with beams
doth blind
mine eye

Her tongue
with sound
doth charm
mine ear

Her wit
with art
doth knit
my heart

Mine eye
with life
her face
doth feed

Mine ear
with hope
her tongue
doth feast

My heart
with skill
her wit
doth fill

O face
with frowns
wrong not
mine eye

O tongue
with cheeks
vex not
mine ear

O wit
with smart
wound not
my heart

This eye
shall joy
her face
to serve

This ear
shall yield
her tongue
to trust

This heart
shall swear
her wit
to fear.

Extract from **The Anniversary**
John Donne (1572–1631)

All Kings, and all their favourites,
All glory of honours, beauties, wits,
The sun itself, which makes times, as they pass,
Is elder by a year now than it was
When thou and I first one another saw:
All other things to their destruction draw,
Only our love hath no decay;
This no tomorrow hath, nor yesterday,
Running it never runs from us away,
But truly keeps his first, last, everlasting day.

A White Rose
John Boyle O'Reilly (1844–1890)

The red rose whispers of passion,
And the white rose breathes of love;
O the red rose is a falcon,
And the white rose is a dove.

But I send you a cream-white rosebud
With a flush on its petal tips;
For the love that is purest and sweetest
Has a kiss of desire on the lips.

I Knew That I had Been Touched by Love
Author Unknown

*I knew that I had been touched by love the first time I saw you,
and I felt your warmth, and I heard your laughter.
I knew that I had been touched by love when I was hurting from
something that happened, and you came along and made the
hurt go away.
I knew that I had been touched by love when I stopped making
plans with my friends,
and started dreaming dreams with you.
I knew that I had been touched by love when I suddenly stopped
thinking in terms of 'me' and started thinking in terms of 'we'.
I knew that I had been touched by love when suddenly I couldn't
make decisions by myself anymore,
and I had the strong desire to share everything with you.
I knew that I had been touched by love the first time we spent
alone together, and I knew that I wanted to stay with you forever
because I had never felt this touched by love.*

Extract from **A Native American Wedding Ceremony**
Author Unknown

May the sun bring you new happiness by day;
May the moon softly restore you by night;
May the rain wash away your worries
And the breeze blow new strength into your being,
And all the days of your life
May you walk gently through the world and know its beauty.
Now you will feel no rain,
For each of you will be warmth for the other.
Now there will be no more loneliness.

Tribal Wish of the Iroquois Indian
Author Unknown

May you have a safe tent
And no sorrow as you travel.
May happiness attend you in all your paths.
May you keep a heart like the morning,
And may you come slow to the four corners
Where man says goodnight.

Apache Blessing
Author Unknown

*Now you will feel no rain, for each of you will be
shelter for each other.
Now you will feel no cold, for each of you will be the
warmth for the other.
Now you are two persons, but there is only one life before.
Go now to your dwelling place to enter into the days
of your life together.
And may your days be good and long upon the earth.*

*Treat yourselves and each other with respect, and remind
yourselves often of what brought you together. Give the highest
priority to the tenderness, gentleness and kindness that your
connection deserves. When frustration, difficulty and fear assail
your relationship — as they threaten all relationships at one time
or another — remember to focus on what is right between you,
not only the part which seems wrong. In this way, you can ride
out the storms when clouds hide the face of the sun in your lives
— remembering that even if you lose sight of it for a moment, the
sun is still there. And if each of you takes responsibility for the
quality of your life together, it will be marked by abundance
and delight.*

Only our Love
John Donne (1572-1631)

Only our love hath no decay;
This, no tomorrow hath, nor yesterday,
Running it never runs from us away,
But truly keeps his first, last, everlasting day

Extract from
Lines composed a few miles above Tintern Abbey
William Wordsworth (1770-1850)

The best portion of a good man's life,
His little, nameless, unremembered acts,
Of kindness and of love.

Love is Enough
William Morris (1834-1896)

Love is enough: though the World be a-waning,
And the woods have no voice but the voice of complaining,
Though the sky be too dark for dim eyes to discover
The gold-cups and daisies fair blooming thereunder,
Though the hills be held shadows, and the sea a dark wonder
And this day draw a veil over all deeds pass'd over,
Yet their hands shall not tremble, their feet shall not falter;
The void shall not weary, the fear shall not alter
These lips and these eyes of the loved and the lover.

Love and Age
Thomas Love Peacock (1785–1866)

I play'd with you' mid cowslips blowing,
When I was six and you were four;
When garlands weaving, flower-balls throwing,
Were pleasures soon to please no more.
Through groves and meads, o'er grass and heather,
With little playmates to and fro,
We wander'd hand in hand together;
But that was sixty years ago.

You grew a lovely roseate maiden,
And still our early love was strong;
Still with no care our days were laden,
They glided joyously along;
And I did love you very dearly,
How dearly words want power to show;
I thought your heart was touch'd as nearly;
But that was fifty years ago.

Then other lovers came around you,
Your beauty grew from year to year,
And many a splendid circle found you
The centre of its glittering sphere.
I saw you then, first vows forsaking,
On rank and wealth your hand bestow;
O, then I thought my heart was breaking! –
But that was forty years ago.

And I lived on, to wed another:
No cause she gave me to repine;
And when I heard you were a mother,
I did not wish the children mine.
My own young flock, in fair progression,
Made up a pleasant Christmas row:
My joy in them was past expression;
But that was thirty years ago.

You grew a matron plump and comely,
You dwelt in fashion's brightest blaze;
My earthly lot was far more homely;
But I too had my festal days.
No merrier eyes have ever glisten'd
Around the hearth-stone's wintry glow,
Than when my youngest child was christen'd:
But that was twenty years ago.

Time pass'd. My eldest girl was married,
And I am now a grandsire gray;
One pet of four years old I've carried
Among the wild-flower'd meads to play.
In our old fields of childish pleasure,
Where now, as then, the cowslips blow,
She fills her basket's ample measure;
And that is not ten years ago.

A Walled Garden
Author Unknown

*'Your marriage', he said, 'Should have within it
A secret and protected place, open to you alone.
Imagine it to be a walled garden.
Entered by a door to which only you have the key.
Within this garden you will cease to be a mother,
father, employee,
Homemaker or any other roles which you fulfil in daily life.
Here you are yourselves, two people who love each other.
Here you can concentrate on one another's needs.
So take my hand and let us go back to our garden.
The time we spend together is not wasted but invested.
Invested in our future and the nurture of our love.'*

(untitled)
Rumi (1207–1273)

*The minute I heard my first love story
I started looking for you, not knowing
how blind that was.*

*Lovers don't finally meet somewhere.
They're in each other all along.*

The Day
Author Unknown

*May this be the start of a happy new life
that's full of special moments to share
May this be the first of your dreams come true
and of hope that will always be there...
May this be the start of a lifetime of trust
and of caring that's just now begun...*

*May today be a day that you'll always remember
the day when your hearts become one...*

Wedding Day
Author Unknown

*Now comes the knitting, the tying, the entwining into one,
Mysterious involvement of two, whole separate people
Into something altogether strange and changing and lovely.
Nothing can ever be, we will never be the same again;
Not merged into each other irrevocably but rather
From now on we go the same way, in the same direction,
Agreeing not to leave each other lonely, or discouraged or behind,
I will do my best to keep my promises to you and keep you warm;
And we will make our wide bed beneath the bright and ragged quilt
of all the yesterdays that make us who we are,
The strengths and frailties we bring to this marriage,
And we will be rich indeed.*

On Your Wedding Day
Author Unknown

Today is a day you will always remember
The greatest in anyone's life
You'll start off the day just two people in love
And end it as Husband and Wife

It's a brand new beginning the start of a journey
With moments to cherish and treasure
And although there'll be times when you both disagree
These will surely be outweighed by pleasure

You'll have heard many words of advice in the past
When the secrets of marriage were spoken
But you know that the answers lie hidden inside
Where the bond of true love lies unbroken

So live happy forever as lovers and friends
It's the dawn of a new life for you
As you stand there together with love in your eyes
From the moment you whisper 'I do'

And with luck, all your hopes, and your dreams can be real
May success find it's way to your hearts
Tomorrow can bring you the greatest of joys
But today is the day it all starts.

What is Love
Author unknown

Sooner or later we begin to understand that love is more than verses on valentines and romance in the movies. We begin to know that love is here and now, real and true, the most important thing in our lives. For love is the creator of our favourite memories and the foundation of our fondest dreams. Love is a promise that is always kept, a fortune that can never be spent, a seed that can flourish in even the most unlikely of places. And this radiance that never fades, this mysterious and magical joy, is the greatest treasure of all – one known only by those who love.

$$\female + \male = \, ?$$

Extract from *The Velveteen Rabbit*
Margery Williams (1881–1944)

'What is REAL?' asked the Rabbit one day, when they were lying side by side near the nursery fender, before Nana came to tidy the room. 'Does it mean having things that buzz inside you and a stick-out handle?'

'Real isn't how you are made,' said the Skin Horse. 'It's a thing that happens to you. When someone loves you for a long, long time, not just to play with, but REALLY loves you, then you become Real.'

'Does it hurt?' asked the Rabbit.

'Sometimes,' said the Skin Horse, for he was always truthful. 'When you are Real you don't mind being hurt.'

'Does it happen all at once, like being wound up,' he asked, 'or bit by bit?'

'It doesn't happen all at once,' said the Skin Horse. 'You become. It takes a long time. That's why it doesn't happen often to people who break easily, or have sharp edges, or who have to be carefully kept. Generally, by the time you are Real, most of your hair has been loved off, and your eyes drop out and you get loose in your joints and very shabby. But these things don't matter at all, because once you are Real you can't be ugly, except to people who don't understand.'

'I suppose you are real?' said the Rabbit. And then he wished he had not said it, for he thought the Skin Horse might be sensitive. But the Skin Horse only smiled.

'Someone made me Real,' he said. 'That was a great many years ago; but once you are Real you can't become unreal again. It lasts for always.'

Marriage Advice
Jane Wells (1886)

Let your love be stronger than your hate or anger.
Learn the wisdom of compromise, for it is better to bend
a little than to break.
Believe the best rather than the worst.
People have a way of living up or down to your opinion
of them.
Remember that true friendship is the basis for any lasting
relationship.
The person you choose to marry is deserving of the
courtesies and kindnesses you bestow on your friends.
Please hand this down to your children and your
children's children.

Our Family
Author unknown

Our family is a circle of love and strength.
With every birth and every union, the circle grows.
Every joy shared adds more love.
Every obstacle faced together makes the circle stronger.

Readings for the reception

You may like to have a short reading at your reception before you sit down to the wedding breakfast, or to introduce the speeches.

From this day Forward
Author unknown

From this day forward,
You shall not walk alone.
My heart will be your shelter,
And my arms will be your home.

These I can Promise
Author Unknown

I cannot promise you a life of sunshine;
I cannot promise riches, wealth, or gold;
I cannot promise you an easy pathway
That leads away from change or growing old.

But I can promise all my heart's devotion;
A smile to chase away your tears of sorrow;
A love that's ever true and ever growing;
A hand to hold in yours through each tomorrow.

Our Mother
Author Unknown

You are the mother I received
The day I wed your son.
And I just want to thank you, Mum
For all the things you've done.

You've given me a gracious man
With whom I share my life.
You are his loving mother and
I his lucky wife.

You used to pat his little head,
And now I hold his hand.
You raised in love a little boy
And gave to me a man.

A Valentine to my Wife
Eugene Field (1850–1895)

Accept, dear girl, this little token,
And if between the lines you seek,
You'll find the love I've often spoken –
The love my dying lips shall speak.
Our little ones are making merry
O'er am'rous ditties rhymed in jest,
But in these words (though awkward – very)
The genuine article's expressed.
You are as fair and sweet and tender,
Dear brown-eyed little sweetheart mine,
As when, a callow youth and slender,
I asked to be your Valentine.
What though these years of ours be fleeting?
What though the years of youth be flown?
I'll mock old Tempus with repeating,
"I love my love and her alone!"
And when I fall before his reaping,
And when my stuttering speech is dumb,
Think not my love is dead or sleeping,
But that it waits for you to come.
So take, dear love, this little token,
And if there speaks in any line
The sentiment I'd fain have spoken,
Say, will you kiss your Valentine?

My True Love Hath my Heart
Sir Philip Sidney (1554–1586)

My true-love hath my heart, and I have his,
By just exchange one for another given:
I hold his dear, and mine he cannot miss,
There never was a better bargain driven:

My true-love hath my heart, and I have his,
My heart in me keeps him and me in one,
My heart in him his thoughts and senses guide:
He loves my heart, for once it was his own,
I cherish his because in me it bides:

My true-love hath my heart, and I have his.

This Day I Married my Best Friend
Author Unknown

This day I married my best friend
…the one I laugh with as we share life's wondrous zest,
as we find new enjoyments and experience all that's best.
…the one I live for because the world seems brighter
as our happy times are better and our burdens feel much lighter.
…the one I love with every fibre of my soul.
We used to feel vaguely incomplete, now together we are whole.

First Love
John Clare (1793–1864)

*I ne'er was struck before that hour
With love so sudden and so sweet.
Her face it bloomed like a sweet flower
And stole my heart away complete.*

*My face turned pale, a deadly pale.
My legs refused to walk away,
And when she looked, what could I ail?
My life and all seemed turned to clay.*

*And then my blood rushed to my face
And took my eyesight quite away,
The trees and bushes round the place
Seemed midnight at noonday.*

I could not see a single thing,
Words from my eyes did start –
They spoke as chords do from the string,
And blood burnt round my heart.

Are flowers the winter's choice?
Is love's bed always snow?
She seemed to hear my silent voice,
Not love appeals to know.

I never saw so sweet a face
As that I stood before.
My heart has left its dwelling-place
And can return no more.

Wedding vows

Doing it your own way

Although there are statutory phrases in both civil and church ceremonies that must be said in order for a marriage to be contracted, there is increasingly more scope, and more demand by brides and grooms, for personalized vows at weddings.

Children, family and friends and humour can all also be included when personalizing your own vows.

This section of the book aims to give you some suggestions and assistance in creating your own promises for marriage.

Writing your own vows for a civil ceremony

Personalizing your vows is especially relevant for couples choosing a civil ceremony or those who are not tying the knot for the first time. If you are choosing a civil ceremony, personalized vows may be used to inject personality and a unique flavour into the wedding. If one or both of you are getting married for the second time, writing your own vows is a way to make the ceremony different, and special to this new union.

Writing your own vows for a civil ceremony

If you are getting married by civil ceremony in the United Kingdom – for example, in a register office or an approved premises – then you may be allowed to include your own choice of vows in addition to the statutory words that legally bind you as husband and wife. Although there is nothing in law to prevent you from including your own vows, some registrars have fixed views about what they will and will not permit. If your registrar will not allow you much freedom, you can ask to have another registrar appointed (from the same register office) who may be more flexible, but don't leave it till the last minute. In all cases, your registrar has the final say.

The statutory words

The minimum vows required for your marriage to be legal are as follows. These words must be said by both of you in your ceremony. You will usually be allowed to add your own choice of vows before or after the statutory ones.

In England and Wales the statutory declaration is:
I do solemnly declare that I know not of any lawful impediment why I, ____, may not be joined in matrimony to ____.

It is followed by these contracting words:
I call upon these persons here present to witness that I, ____, do take thee, ____, to be my lawful wedded husband/wife.

There are also two legal alternative declarations.

Declaration: *I know of no legal reason why I, ____, may not be joined in marriage to ____.*

Or by replying 'I am' to the question: *Are you, ____, free lawfully to marry ____?*

These are followed by the contract:
I, ____, take you, ____ to be my wedded wife/husband.
or
I, ____, take thee, ____ to be my wedded wife/husband.

In Scotland the couple say:
I solemnly declare that I know of no legal impediment why I, ____, may not be joined in matrimony to ____. I accept.

In Northern Ireland the statutory declaration is:
I know of no lawful impediment why I, ____, may not be joined in matrimony to, ____, to be my lawful wedded husband/wife.

Writing your vows for a humanist ceremony

If you are looking for an even more personalized wedding ceremony in a civil venue or even in a beautiful garden or marquee, then think about a humanist wedding. This is a non-denominational celebration of a couple's love for each other and the bride and groom can write, or have influence over, every word of the ceremony. (You will also have to have a legally binding civil ceremony at the same time or earlier.)

An official humanist celebrant will provide you with some examples of a standard ceremony and help you to decide which element you wish to include for your big day. You can then add or adapt words depending on what you want to say.

How to decide what to say

There may be elements of your relationship that are more important than others, and the most successful way to write personalized vows is to think about the two of you and the things you would like to promise each other.

You may want to emphasize your underlying friendship for each other, or talk about the fun you can cram into the next few decades. At the other end of the scale, if you have come together after a period of separation, then trust and fidelity are important things to promise to each other. Don't be afraid to have some fun: you might want to make promises about more light-hearted subjects, such as sharing the washing up or keeping the house tidy – although these are usually more appropriate for a humanist ceremony.

Points to remember when writing your vows

Do remember that, at the very heart of your vows, is the fact that this is a public declaration of your commitment to each other. The words should be created for others to witness and not simply as a private conversation between you and your partner.

Do not embarrass your witnesses with over-intimate details or bore them with a lengthy monologue!

Keep your vows short. The art is to express much in a few short, well-chosen statements.

Your vows should include a promise to accept changes and a pledge to grow together during the experiences of a lifetime's partnership. Respecting your partner's right to grow and develop spiritually and mentally during the course of your relationship is a basic necessity for a happy marriage.

Sincerity is the key to meaningful vows. Your words will have a profound effect on your guests. Even guests who are unsure of the wisdom of an alternative ceremony will not be able to find fault with vows that so obviously come from the heart.
Decide whether you each wish to write your own vows separately or whether you both wish to repeat the same vows.

Consider whether you want to include responses from your guests after your vows, asking them to give their blessing to your marriage and to support your relationship in the future.

When you have written your vows, discuss them with the celebrant who is to conduct your ceremony. He or she may have helpful suggestions to make or foresee any problems that may occur. Remember that a professional such as a humanist celebrant is trained and experienced and will have a wealth of knowledge that may help you create the perfect ceremony.

Practise your vows with your partner or a trusted friend.

Make a copy of your vows to have with you during the ceremony or repeat them after the celebrant. Nerves play havoc with the memory and the last thing you want to do is to be worried about whether or not you will remember your words.

Remember to speak slowly and clearly. You are asking your guests to witness your marriage and they need to hear your words.

Whether expressed in your own words or adapting existing ones, most vows follow a simple format: a declaration from each partner that he or she is willing and free to marry; and a commitment from each partner to love and care for each other whatever the future may bring.

What you might include in your vows

Look for inspiration from traditional vows that have stood the test of time. They contain moving and simple words that have forged marriages from generation to generation. They express in a nutshell the key promises upon which a happy marriage can be founded.

Jot down words and phrases from books, films or poetry that touch your heart and express your thoughts. Discuss the special moments in your relationships, whether happy, sad or humorous, to inspire personal meaning in the words you choose. The perfect vows demand the perfect vocabulary. Searching for words and phrases to match the depths of our emotions can be very frustrating. The following words and phrases will help you, but remember the final outcome has to come from the heart and from the bonds that exist between you and your partner.

Promises

To share the good and the bad parts of life together.

To love, honour, respect and cherish each other.

To respect each other's individuality.

To be kind, trusting, tolerant and understanding.

To be honest and faithful.

To stay together for life.

To bring happiness and laughter into the marriage.

To be a good friend.

To create a loving and stable relationship.

Personal attributes

Beauty, Candour, Charisma, Charm, Cheerfulness, Chivalry, Courage, Dependability, Determination, Elegance, Fidelity, Generosity, Gentleness, Grace, Honesty, Humility, Humour, Independence, Innocence, Integrity, Loyalty, Playfulness, Purity, Sense of Humour, Simplicity, Sincerity, Sweetness, Tenderness, Trust, Virtue, Worth

Personal descriptions

Ally, Angel, Beloved, Companion, Darling, Dearest, Friend, Goddess, Hero, Lover, Mate, Partner, Play-fellow, Soulmate, Sweetheart, Treasure

Adjectives

Absolute, Adorable, Alive, Amiable, Appealing, Ardent,
Attractive, Beautiful, Binding, Blameless, Caring, Charming,
Chivalrous, Complete, Considerate, Constant, Courageous,
Cosy, Dauntless, Deserving, Desirable, Devoted, Ecstatic,
Embracing, Emotional, Enduring, Energetic, Entire, Entrancing,
Excellent, Exciting, Fair, Faithful, Fervent, Forgiving, Formal,
Fragile, Gallant, Genuine, Good-humoured, Glorious,
Growing, Happy, Hopeful, High-principled, High-spirited,
Innocent, Jubilant, Lasting, Lively, Lovely, Mutual, Noble,
Popular, Praiseworthy, Precious, Predestined, Reliable,
Romantic, Safe, Secluded, Seductive, Sensational, Sensual,
Significant, Sincere, Snug, Soft, Solemn, Staunch, Stimulating,
Sweet, Triumphant, Unconditional, Upright, Virtuous,
Vivacious, Wonderful, Worthy

Verbs

Affirm, Appreciate, Aspire, Assert, Commit, Confide,
Desire, Declare, Embrace, Endeavour, Entrust, Pledge,
Proclaim, Promise, Protect, Reassure, Seek, Strive, Swear,
Understand, Wonder

Negative Words

Adversity, Anger, Desolation, Despair, Emptiness, Failure,
Fears, Frailty, Jealousy, Neglect, Pressure, Poverty, Problems,
Sickness, Sorrow, Suspicion, Weakness

Phrases

A measure of my love
A relationship built on love and honesty
A symbol of love
All the days of my life
As this ring surrounds your finger, so my love surrounds you
Bonds of love
Cherish, love and comfort
Companion in joy and comfort in adversity
Dearer than life itself
For an eternity of tomorrows
Friend, love and protector
From the depths of my heart
Give myself to you
Give you room to grow
Heart of my heart
I do not expect you to fulfil all my dreams, only to share
them and allow me to share yours
In sickness and in health
In sunshine and in shadow
In the presence of our friends and family I stand before you

Sample vows

I promise to love and respect you and to put energy into keeping our love alive. I will be there for you in good times and bad. I will help you when you need help and make space for you to be yourself. I will try to bring you happiness.

I will dedicate myself to you wholeheartedly. I will make time for you and support you in everything you do. I will help you to raise our children to become loving people, and support you in the fundamental role of parent.

I pledge my life to you. I will love, honour and respect you in happy and sad times. I promise to be faithful to only you as long as we both live.

I, _____ _____, promise to love and cherish you, _____ _____, for the rest of your life. I will try to bring laughter to your life, and make you happy. I will consider you in the decisions I have to make, and value your opinions. Today I vow to be your husband/wife for the rest of our lives.

I will seek to always be loving unto you. I will share your joys and your sorrows, and will be devoted unto you until the ultimate parting.

_____, I _____, take you to be my husband/wife. To have to hold from this day forward, for better, for worse, for richer for poorer, in sickness and in health, to love and to cherish till death us do part, and this is my solemn vow.

_____ _____, today I promise to respect you always. I will share the good times and bad times with you, be a support and guide. Above all, I will love you from now until our days end.

I, _____ _____, promise to be to you, _____ _____, a true and loving companion. I promise to be the best husband/wife and parent that I can be and to commit myself forever to our relationship together.

Today I promise to you to be your husband/wife. I will be faithful and honest, loving and trustworthy. I will seek to bring you stability and order in a chaotic world. I will be your partner and friend for life.

_____, in this beautiful garden I dedicate myself to you. Although our lives may change like the seasons, I will love you. As our love grows like a seed to a beautiful flower, I will love you. When the winds of doubt blow through, I will love you. We will stand together, strong, nurtured by each other's love until the end.

Vows that include children

If there are children involved in your relationship then it is a nice touch to include them in your wedding vows, either by mentioning them by name, or giving them their own special lines to say.

GROOM: *Today, _____, I ask you to be my wife. To be loving, tolerant and loyal, supporting me in my life. I ask that you vow to do your best for our relationship, for our children and for our lives together. Will you promise this?*

BRIDE: *I will. And I ask you, _____, to be my husband. To be devoted and faithful, loving and supporting me and working for the good of our relationship and our family. Will you promise this?*

GROOM: *I will.*

REGISTRAR/CELEBRANT: *As _____ and _____ come together as husband and wife, they create a new family. The children of _____ and _____ are now going to ask for a promise from their parents.*

CHILDREN *(together or taking one line each): Will you accept us as part of your family together? Will you love and care for us? Will you guide us and support us?*

BRIDE AND GROOM: *We will.*

REGISTRAR/CELEBRANT: *Today, _____, _____ and their children have made a new family, and together they promise to consider each other, to be loving, respectful and devoted to each other.*

Here are some other examples:

I pledge today that I will be a loving and devoted husband/wife to you, and a loving and devoted parent to ____ and ____.

In front of our children I promise to keep only to you for as long as we both shall live.

I, ____, take you, ____, to be my lawful wedded wife and your children, ____ and ____, to be our family.

I look forward to spending the rest of my life with you and our children, ____ and ____, sharing the good times, supporting you through the bad.

I offer myself to you as a partner in life, and to our children as a parent.

I promise to accept the responsibility of being a loving and guiding parent to your children.

From this day forward, I make this solemn vow, that I will always be there for you and our children, in sickness and in health, for richer or poorer, till death do us part.

Vows that include your guests

I,_____, in front of our friends and family, promise to...

I, _____, take you, _____, to be my husband/wife, in front of all our witnesses.

I ask everyone present to witness that I openly take _____ to be my wife/husband.

I ask everyone present to witness that I promise to spend my life with _____.

Here today, in front of our family and friends, I take you, _____, to be my wife/husband.

I thank our friends and family for gathering here today to witness our marriage.

Your celebrant can also include your guests in your ceremony.

REGISTRAR/CELEBRANT: Will you, the friends and family of _____ and _____, support them in their marriage, lend them every help in their life together and be a constant reminder of the vows they have made here in front of you today?

CONGREGATION: We will.

REGISTRAR/CELEBRANT: _____ and _____ are now embarking on married life. Before you they have given their consent to each other, and made solemn vows. They now ask that you will give them your love and support in their new life together.

CONGREGATION: We will.

Vows that follow a question and answer format

If you are confident about your ability to learn your vows you may prefer to recite them while making eye contact with each other. However, if you feel that your nerves will get the better of you and that you will clam up or, worse still, get a fit of the giggles, you may prefer to read them from a card. Alternatively your registrar or celebrant can read out your vows for you to repeat. Many of the preceding vows can also be structured in this way.

REGISTRAR/CELEBRANT: _____ _____, *today you have come to promise to share you life with* _____ _____. *Do you promise to love and protect her, to be faithful to her and to be always supporting and understanding?*
Do you promise to share your life with each other, to trust and be honest and faithful to each other? Will you live in a spirit of tolerance, mutual support and concern for each other's well being, sharing your responsibilities and joys?

GROOM: *I do*

REGISTRAR/CELEBRANT: *We have come together today to witness the vows that* _____ *and* _____ *are about to make.* _____ *do you now agree to take* _____ *as your wife, understanding and expecting that she will be your partner for life? Will you love her, support her and help her to achieve her potential? Will you share your love through whatever is to come, until the end of your life?*

GROOM: *I will*

Vows for fun

Your wedding vows can be as amusing and tongue-in-cheek as they can be serious, and can reflect any aspect of your relationship. So go on – have some fun! If your registrar disapproves or you would rather stick to something more solemn for your wedding ceremony, you could always use your alternative vows during the reception speeches. Here are a few ideas to get you started…

GROOM: *I promise to put the top on the toothpaste, my dirty washing in the laundry basket and not to clean my football boots on the kitchen table. Oh, and to love you always.*

BRIDE: *I promise to learn to cook something other than baked beans on toast, not to hog the bathroom and use all the hot water, and never to ask 'Does my bum look big in this?' and expect an honest answer.*

GROOM: *I pledge to do my share of the dusting, the hoovering, the cooking, the washing up, making the bed, cleaning the bathroom, the ironing, moving the lawn, walking the dog, washing the car, decorating the house and – if I am still physically able at the end of the day – to love you.*

BRIDE: *I promise to care for you in sickness and in health, unless it is self-inflicted and two o'clock in the morning; not to hit you too hard when you are snoring; to let you in after a night out with the lads; and to care for your prize collection of beer mats.*

GROOM: *I vow to understand you when I don't; to admit that I am in the wrong when I mistakenly think I am in the right; and to bring you flowers at least once a week as I am bound to have done something that I should apologize for.*

BRIDE: *I promise not to phone my mum more than seven times a week, to buy only one pair of shoes a month and to accept all your bad habits as being what makes you as lovable as you are.*

With this ring I thee wed...

Exchanging rings is not a legal necessity for marriage, but if you choose to do so, then you may want to consider the wording you will use. The Church of England wording is:

MINISTER: *Heavenly Father, by your blessing let these rings be to ____ and ___ a symbol of unending love and faithfulness, to remind them of the vow and covenant which they have made this day, through Jesus Christ our Lord, Amen.*

As the groom places the ring on the bride's third finger of her left hand, he says:
_____, I give you this ring as a sign of our marriage. With my body I honour you, all that I am I give to you and all that I have I share with you, within the love of God, Father, Son and Holy Spirit.

Non-religious options

I give you this ring as a symbol of our marriage and of my enduring love.

This ring symbolizes our relationship, which is whole and without end.

*Our separate lives come together and are eternally one.
The inside of this ring symbolizes our love for each other in our union and the outside the world that we participate in as one.*

Accepting and receiving the ring

*I give you this ring as a symbol that part of me will forever be a part of you.
I accept this ring as a symbol that part of you is forever a part of me.
With this ring I give you my love as we journey through life together.
I accept this ring as a precious symbol of your love, which is always with me on our journey.*

An alternatives to rings

This candle is a token of our future life together, and the hopes and aspirations that we share.

The light of this candle burns as brightly as our future together and as strongly as our love for each other.

Outlining your vows

Use this exercise to help you work out what you want to say in your vows. You and your partner should complete the first part separately. When you have written down all your ideas, swap papers and read through each other's. Make a note of your favourite bits of both, and use this as the basis for writing your vows together.

Write down the following:
• Ten words that describe your partner
• Ten words that describe your relationship
• A time when you both laughed so much you cried
• A time when you were unhappy and your partner was there for you
• How you felt when you first realized you were in love with your partner
• A short paragraph picturing your life together in 30 years time
• The names of any poems or readings you like, and what particularly appeals to you about them
• Any song lyrics that reflect how you feel about your relationship
• What marriage means to you
• If relevant, what having a family means to you
• Note down any 'themes' that recur. These may relate to a second marriage, getting married later in life, a particular event that has shaped your life together, or even your jobs

Structuring your vows

When you have decided what to say in your vows, you need to structure them into an introduction, middle and end. Here are some examples.

Introduction

I, _____, take you _____, for my lifelong husband/wife.

I, _____, take you _____, as my partner on life's journey.

I, _____, take you _____, to be my wife/husband, best friend, comforter and soulmate.

I, _____, choose you _____, to be my partner for life.

Then follow with the main body of your vows.

Ending

This is my solemn promise to you.

I promise this to you today, tomorrow and forever.

I will share my life with you for as long as we both shall live.

From this moment on, this is my true promise to you.

Come what may, this shall remain my promise to you.

Renewing your vows

Vow renewal is gaining popularity in this country. Although the various churches do offer vow renewal ceremonies, couples often take this opportunity to have a more flexible ceremony, including many personal aspects of their life together.

If you are considering writing your own vows for a renewal ceremony, there are three aspects you might like to include. The first is your life together since you first made your vows to each other. What were the highlights? Buying your first home, travelling round the world, the birth of your children? How did your spouse make those experiences even more important for you? How do you specifically remember your spouse at these times? What were the low points and how did you overcome them together? What did you learn about your spouse during this time?

Then look at your original vows. Do you think they have reflected your married life fairly since you made them? Which of them have you both truly kept? Which of them do you think you are still working at?

Finally, consider your future together. What are your hopes and dreams? How does this differ from the future you envisaged when you first made your vows? What are you going to do differently from now on, and what are you going to keep the same?

You might like to start by saying: 'We stand here today before family and friends as we have stood here before. In front of them I again take...' Or 'Ten years from the day on which we were first joined together, my faith in this marriage is stronger than ever. The years we have spent together have given me the joy with which I promise again to be your husband/wife.'

Getting married abroad

If you choose to get married abroad, whether you can use your own vows or not will depend on the country and religion. For instance, in the Bahamas you can get married in church or in a civil ceremony. If you contact your registrar in advance, it may be possible to discuss adding your own vows to the civil ceremony. The US is very flexible as to vows, but if you're going to get married by Elvis or a NYC judge, don't expect to get more than the standard declarations. However, for a more elaborate arrangement you'll be expected to write your own personalized statements.

If you're getting married in Europe, the ceremony will be in the native language. Bear in mind they won't be a direct translation of the UK vows. You do have to understand the vows you are making, so if you don't want a translator, then it is advisable to obtain a copy of the vows from your co-ordinator or the embassy beforehand, in order to familiarize yourself with the wording of the promises you will be making.

Summing up

Whatever you decide, the most important element of your vows is sincerity. Write your vows from the heart and speak from the heart on the day. As you say them, try to focus on the meaning of every word and remember why you have chosen to make those particular vows to your partner.

On a practical note, try to speak clearly and loudly because your guests will be eager to hear what you have to say. Some people make photocopies of their vows to distribute among guests. This will enable your family and friends to read along as the ceremony progresses and will also give them a souvenir of your wedding.

Make a copy of your vows for a keepsake box, or frame one and display it with your wedding photographs. You will always be able to look back at what you promised one another on your wedding day.

Literary Acknowledgments

Permission to quote Kahlil Gibran's poem 'On Marriage' and from 'The Prophet' was granted by the Gibran National Committee, P.O. Box 116-5375, Beirut, Lebanon
phone and fax: (+961-1) 676916;
e-mail: k.gibran@cyberia.net.lb

Scripture quotations taken from the Holy Bible, New International Version. Copyright © 1973, 1978, 1984 by International Bible Society. Used by permission of Hodder & Stoughton Ltd., a member of the Hodder Headline Plc Group. All rights reserved.

Every effort has been made to trace copyright holders. We apologize for any unintentional omission and would be pleased to insert an acknowledgement in subsequent editions.

Confetti.co.uk is the UK's leading wedding and special occasion website, helping more than 300,000 brides, grooms and guests every month.

Easy to use, the confetti.co.uk website is packed full of ideas and advice to help organize every stage of your wedding. You can choose from hundreds of beautiful wedding dresses; investigate our list of more than 3,000 wedding and reception venues; plan your wedding; chat to other brides about their experiences and ask for advice from Aunt Betti, our agony aunt. We will even help you set up a website, for you to share details and photos online with family and friends.

Our extensive online content on every aspect of weddings and special occasions is now complemented by our range of books covering every aspect of planning a wedding, for everyone involved. Titles include *Wedding Planner, Confettiquette, How to Write a Wedding Speech, Wedding Speeches* and mini books *Wedding Readings, Men at Weddings, The Best Man's Wedding, The Bridesmaid's Wedding, Your Daughter's Wedding, The Wedding Book of Calm, Compatibility* and *Wedding Trivia.*

confetti also offer:

Wedding Gifts – there's something for everyone in our exciting range, including American retro and diner furniture, homeware and accessories from Jerry's Home Store
Wedding Stationary – our stunning ranges include all the pieces you will need
Wedding and Party Products – stocking everything you need from streamers to candles to cameras to cards to flowers to fireworks and, of course, confetti!

To find out more or to order your confetti gift book, party brochure or wedding stationery brochure:
visit: www.confetti.co.uk
call: 0870 840 6060
email: info@confetti.co.uk
visit: Confetti, 80 Tottenham Court Road, London W1